The 100 Most Powerful Morning Prayers Every Christian Needs to Know

Get your life straightened, your faith strengthened, your wisdom raised, your satisfaction fulfilled, your joy ripened and happiness delivered through these 100 powerful prayers now!

D0452125

Introduction

Praying to God is not at all an "option"! It is as essential as it is essential to breathe because the air we breathe in and our organs of breathing are all blessings of God. So, can't we just take out a few minutes of our busy, stressed out lives to thank Him? If he has the power to create us, take back our souls, and to raise us from the death-bed on the day of judgement, doesn't he have the power to solve our daily problems? So, why not turn to our Lord if we want something? He is immensely powerful, mighty and at the same time, He is merciful, loving and caring. He wants us to pray to him as much as we want to pray to him, because that is what maintains the relationship between the devotee and his/her God.

If God has created a problem, he has created solution for it too. If there is a lock, there is a key too. So, if your life is locked in some issue, or you feel you need some shower of blessings for some asset in your life, the prayers are the keys – the keys that open doors of the immense treasures of our Lord.

Why should we pray?

- To give thanks to our Lord for everything he has bestowed us with
- To renew our soul
- To grow in our heart the seeds of love
- To ask Him for the help in various walks of life
- To ask him for blessing us with virtues
- To pray for the well being of others
- To seek His forgiveness after we commit a sin as he is the merciful and forgiving Lord
- Because Christ asked us to pray.

Make Your Life a Continuous Prayer

God wants us to live a life of a constant prayer, the life in which even our work becomes worship as we keep following what he has ordered for us in all our dealings.

How to use this book?

We are so lost in our personal dealings that we find it very cumbersome to go to Church. We procrastinate and procrastinate, and in this procrastinating menace, we forget our God when we look back at our lives. If we just make a habit of using one prayer a day as mentioned in this book, with our full mind and concentration, focussing on every single word of the prayer, our lives will become phenomenal.

Don't worry about the days when you wouldn't get free time (hey do we need to worship God in our free time only?... think!), but make sure that you have used one prayer/your favourite prayer from this book before you sleep. Preferably pray in the morning, because that way your day will glow with the holiness of your Lord. However, do make it a habit to use at least one prayer a day. This way, your connection with your Lord will automatically grow so strong that you would have memorized the wordings of the prayer and whenever you would feel helpless, whenever you would feel depressed, or you want to express gratitude, words would automatically come out of your heart.

How to Pray?

Keep the following things in mind while using the prayers in this book:

- Pray with complete **attention** – so that we can have a true encounter with God
- Pray with total **humility** – because this sort of prayer goes straight to God's ear
- Pray with tears and **affection** in your heart
- Pray the gratitude prayers with a feeling of **satisfaction** and **gratitude** towards your Lord
- Pray with **ardour** and **patience**
- Pray from the **core of your heart**
- Pray with full belief and an **absolute trust in God that your prayer would be answered,** and it would be answered.
- Do not just rush your prayer, no matter how small the prayer is, **Focus on Each and every Word**
- **Feel the power and blessings** after each prayer

This book doesn't just contain daily prayers, but it captures 100 great prayers for the gifts of virtues; for families and similar kinds of relationships; for different activities and events; for important moments in time; against various forms of sin; for righteousness and salvation; and finally for others in difficult situations.

Thank you readers, God bless you and do not forget to once in a while pray for me too as He answers the prayers of His every beloved servant. Remember: Prayers can move mountains. Prayer is the reliever of the heart, the provider of hope and the fortress of resilience against all odds.

© Copyright 2015 by Oliver Powell - All rights reserved.

This document is geared towards providing exact and reliable information in regards to the topic and issue covered. The publication is sold with the idea that the publisher is not required to render accounting, officially permitted, or otherwise, qualified services. If advice is necessary, legal or professional, a practiced individual in the profession should be ordered.

- From a Declaration of Principles which was accepted and approved equally by a Committee of the American Bar Association and a Committee of Publishers and Associations.

In no way is it legal to reproduce, duplicate, or transmit any part of this document in either electronic means or in printed format. Recording of this publication is strictly prohibited and any storage of this document is not allowed unless with written permission from the publisher. All rights reserved.

The information provided herein is stated to be truthful and consistent, in that any liability, in terms of inattention or otherwise, by any usage or abuse of any policies, processes, or directions contained within is the solitary and utter responsibility of the recipient reader. Under no circumstances will any legal responsibility or blame be held against the publisher for any reparation, damages, or monetary loss due to the information herein, either directly or indirectly.

Respective authors own all copyrights not held by the publisher.

The information herein is offered for informational purposes solely, and is universal as so. The presentation of the information is without contract or any type of guarantee assurance.

The trademarks that are used are without any consent, and the publication of the trademark is without permission or backing by the trademark owner. All trademarks and brands within this book are for clarifying purposes only and are the owned by the owners themselves, not affiliated with this document.

Table Of Contents

Part 1

Prayers for the Gift of Virtues

Prayer 1: Prayer for Guidance

"O my Lord,

Open my heart,

to envision the path,

the path that you selected for me

To feel thy rays of light amidst the dark,

to envision where you would lead me.

Open my deaf ears to thy holy voice,

The voice that guides me though the noise

Make my heart so soft that it melts to your grace,

Embrace my soul that it knows where to face

Guide my mind that I comprehend your affection,

Strengthen my legs that they follow your direction,

Till the time I establish my life's purpose,

Till the time I reach my destination,

Then I would have no fear of getting astray,

Like a child whose mother isn't far away!"

Amen!

Prayer 2: Prayer for Unity

"O my Lord, You inspire us to transform our world.

Empower us to seek the common good for all persons.

Give us a spirit of solidarity and make us one human family."

Amen!

Prayer 3: Prayer for Truth

"O my Lord, Your truth is made known in your Word.

Guide us to seek the truth of the human person.

Teach us the way to love because you are Love."

Amen!

Prayer 4: Prayer for Guidance (2)

"I beg you for the light
I so earnestly need
that I may find the way of life
in which lies the best fulfillment of your will.
Whatever state this may be,
give me the grace necessary
to embrace it with love of Your holy will,
I offer myself to You now,
trusting in Your wisdom and love
to direct me in working out my salvation
and in helping others
to know and come close to You,
so that I may find my reward
in union with You forever and ever."

Amen!

Prayer 5: Prayer for guidance – David's Prayer

"O Lord, in the morning you hear my voice;
in the morning I prepare a sacrifice for you and
watch.
For you are not a God who delights in wickedness;
evil may not dwell with you.
The boastful shall not stand before your eyes;
you hate all evildoers.
You destroy those who speak lies;
the Lord abhors the bloodthirsty and deceitful man.
But I, through the abundance of your steadfast love,
will enter your house.
I will bow down toward your holy temple
in the fear of you.
Lead me, O Lord, in your righteousness
because of my enemies;
make your way straight before me."

Amen!

Prayer 6: Prayer for clarity

O God,
"Make your words so clear to me as clear the ice is,

Make your love be like a compass for me that give me direction,

Make your truth be like a signpost to me that brings clarity,

Make your peace a guide for my directions,

Make your hope be like a flag that tells me that I am walking beside you,

Clear my mind of all the distractions that steal me from you,

O God bless me with clarity"

Amen!

Prayer 7: Prayer for Hope

"O my God,

Relying on your infinite mercy and promises,

I hope to obtain pardon of my sins

and the help of your grace."

Amen!

Prayer 8: Prayer for blessings

"May the Lord bless you and keep you.
May the Lord make his face to shine upon you,
and be gracious to you
May the Lord lift up his countenance upon you,
and give you peace."

Amen!

Prayer 9: Prayer for Grace

"O my God! You know my weakness and failings,
and that without your help I can accomplish nothing
for the good of souls, my own and others'. Grant
me, therefore, the help of your grace. Grant it
according to my particular needs this day. Enable
me to see the task you will set before me in the daily
routine of my life, and help me work hard at my
appointed tasks. Teach me to bear patiently all the
trials of suffering or failure that may come to me
today."

Amen!

Prayer 10: Prayer for Grace (2)

"Merciful Lord,

Never stop speaking to my tiny heart,

Grow it up, make it big, fill it with your love, and grant me that grace,

the grace that if I sense your presence today,

my heart is open to embrace the feeling

and not hardened by the vanities of the world"

Amen!

Prayer 11: Prayer for Thanksgiving and commitment

"When I was going astray,

And I had no one else to show way,

I remembered you my caring God,

And my prayer was delivered to you my Lord,

You answered my prayer and gave me what I wanted

All that I cherished for, everything you granted,

I thank you for everything I thank you Oh my Lord,

What I have vowed I will surely pay,

I will sacrifice to you; Salvation belongs to you, my God!"

Amen!

Prayer 12: Prayer for Humility

"O great Lord,
Do restrain my thoughts,
Let them not wander aimlessly,
Amid this world's vanity,
I know I am unworthy,
To be united to your affection,
Still my only desire is to,
Get your loving attention
O Lord Sow in me the deep and fruitful seeds,
of humility, modesty and lack of vanity.
Hide me O my Lord,
Hide me O my God,
Under the wings of your grace
And under your hands of mercy"
Amen!

Prayer 13: Prayer for Perseverance

"Lord as we navigate through this world of sin, thank You that You have promised to be with us, no matter what difficulties and dangers may cross our paths. Keep us we pray, from all perils, problems and persecutions that we may encounter and may we remain firm to the end and enabled to persevere in the midst of all our trials. Thank You that there is no situation in life that is outside of your jurisdiction and that you have every circumstance covered by your sufficient grace. Lord as we steer our path through this sin-sick world may we keep our confidence in you and place every need into your hands, knowing that greater is He that is in us than he that is in the world"

Amen!

Prayer 14: Prayer for Fortitude

"Teach me, O Lord, to bear my sufferings with fortitude and patience."

Amen!

Prayer 15: Prayer for Obedience

"Teach me to do Thy will, because Thou art my God"

Amen!

Prayer 16: Prayers for Courage

"Dear Lord, bless me with courage,
for I want it with full passion.

I want it face all those fierce men to oppose their
threats
and as a force against their seductions.

I want it to bear mockery,

unkindness, and contradiction.

Bless me with courage to wage a war against the
Satan,
against his terrors, against all troubles, and all the
temptations,
Against all attractions, false lights and this
terrorizing darkness,
against all fear, against all tears, and against the
saddening depression.

Your help I need, my Lord!
With your grace, with you love, strengthen my body,
strengthen my mind!

Only Your blessed Presence can console me,
give me the courage to persevere and hold me,
till the day I am with you, my Lord, forever and
forever in the heaven."

Amen!

Prayer 17: Prayer for Oneness

"O Lord, may we be of one mind in truth and of one heart in charity"

Amen!

Prayer 18: Prayer for confidence

"Lord! Give me Your confidence
To trust my God-given capabilities.
Help me with each task at hand
Guide me through its completion."

Amen!

Prayer 19: Prayers against anger

"Lord, May I be slow to anger and filled with love
because you are my hero
and I'm following You."

Amen!

Prayer 20: Prayers for integrity

"My Dear God, we thank you for blessing us with the light of Christ Jesus, who was the perfect example of a man with great character and integrity of spirit. Lord I long to be more like Jesus in all my actions and attitudes and pray that You would guard my heart; strengthen my character; teach me Your ways; uphold me with Your righteous right hand and develop in me the grace and integrity."

Amen!

Prayer 21: Prayer for increasing your impact - Prayer of Jabez

"Oh that you would bless me and enlarge my territory, let your hand be with me, and keep me from harm so that I will be free from pain."

Amen!

Prayer 22: Prayer for purpose in life

"Help me O my Lord,

Help me develop the abundance of joy and a stream of happiness,

a river of eternal peace and an ocean of goodness.

A ray of affection, an array of kindness

A wall of self-control and a bridge of righteousness,

That would establish your purpose of creating me,

May I be a reflection of what you have expected of me,

May I follow the footsteps of Jesus the Christ,

May the seed of love in me grow into a fruitful tree, "

Amen!

Prayer 23: Prayer for Victory - David's Prayer

"To you, O Lord, I lift up my soul. O my God, in you I trust, let me not be put to shame; let not my enemies triumph over me."

Amen!

Prayer 24: Prayer for gratitude

"Thank You for my health and my home. Thank You for my family and my friends. Thank You for the many good gifts that You have been pleased to bestow on all Your children. Thank You Lord, for your guidance, provision of comfort and help - for I am never alone because You are ever by my side ... Praise Your holy name for all the good gifts that You have graciously given me, in such rich abundance"

Amen!

Prayer 25: Prayer for Gratitude (2) - Canticle of the Sun

"Be praised, my Lord,
For all your creatures,
And first for brother sun,
Who makes the day bright and luminous.
He is beautiful and radiant
With great splendor
Be praised, my Lord,
For sister moon and the stars.
You placed them in the sky,
So bright and twinkling"

Amen!

Prayer 26: Prayer for Wisdom

"Oh my Infinite God, Oh Light of the Universe,

You are the giver of Wisdom, You are the source of all Knowledge

You know every-thing before anything is made

You made the light, without which the world is dark,

Bestow us with knowledge, lest in ignorance we bark!

Mend my heart so that it has truthfulness inside

Shape my tongue, so that it utters your praises to the world outside

Inspire my soul with thy grace,

Teach my thoughts to be pure and eyes to be chaste

Fill my existence with infinite Wisdom from your knowledge treasure

So that I take every step only to seek your pleasure "

Amen!

Prayer 27: Prayer for purity

*"Lord, inflame our hearts and our inmost beings
with the fire of your holiness, that we may serve You
with chaste bodies and pure minds."*

Amen!

Prayer 28: Prayer for peace of mind

*"Give me the strength and clarity of mind to find my
purpose and walk the path you've laid out for me. I
trust your Love God, and know that you will heal
this stress. Just as the sun rises each day against the
dark of night, please bring me clarity with your
light."*

Amen!

Prayer 29: Prayer for serenity

*"God grant me the serenity
To accept the things I cannot change;
Courage to change the things I can;
And wisdom to know the difference."*

Amen!

Prayer 30: Prayers for compassion

O Lord bless us with compassion

O Lord bestow our hearts with humility

O God make us gentle, Oh God make us loving,

O God make us generous and giving and forgiving

Kill our pride as you fulfill our dreams,

Turn our boastful tongue into a compassionate mouth organ,

Increase our love for thee

Increase our affection for thee

Amen!

Prayer 31: Prayer for compassion

"Lord, open our eyes
that we may see you in our brothers and sisters.
Lord, open our ears
that we may hear the cries of the hungry,
the cold, the frightened, the oppressed.
Lord, open our hearts
that we may love each other as you love us.
Lord, free us and make us one."
Amen!

Prayer 32: Suscipe

(St. Ignatius of Loyola)

"Take, Lord, and receive all my liberty,
my memory, my understanding,
and my entire will,
All I have and call my own.

You have given all to me.
To you, Lord, I return it.

Everything is yours; do with it what you will.
Give me only your love and your grace,
that is enough for me."

Amen!

Prayer 33: Prayer for mercy

"God, in Thy mercy, in Thy love, Be Thou with us
now. For we know and we speak of Thy love, and
help us then to put away, for the hour, The cares of
this life; that we may know in truth That the spirit
and the lamb say, "Come." Let them that hear also
say, "Come." Let all that will, come and drink of the
water of life."

Amen!

Prayer 34: Prayer for Mercy (2)

"My Lord, have thy mercy on me

My God, wash me out from my iniquity.

Cleanse my soul of every impurity,

Whiter than snow and clearer than ice,

Oh God let my heart be!

Let me walk on the righteous way,

The way that my beloved Jesus laid down for me

You created my seed and the roots of my tree,

I polluted the fruits that as I let my desires roam free.

Oh Lord have mercy, Oh God Have Mercy

And all I want now is to return in pure form unto thee."

Amen!

Prayer 35: A plea for mercy as well as a song of praise

"Oh Lord! Your reputation is high,
Your work is phenomenal,
You are the synonym of perfection,
Before taking a deep sigh of relief,
When I remember,
how great is your power,
how vast is your kingdom,
how unique is your creativity,
how flawless is your design,
how ultimate is the shower,
that you bring down after weeks of sunny days,
to quench the thirst of every single lover,
or even a big sinner,
you are very just,
just like your sun,
that shines on living beings and even on dust,
Oh God, shine your mercy on me,
As I am thirsty,
Thirsty of your holy grace and mercy,
You are my strength,
You are my hope,

You are the one who bestowed us with Jesus,

You are the one the one who made Him the healer,

Oh Lord heal my wounds too,

The wounds of my heart,

Arouse in my heart the love for you,

Love for Jesus and love for humanity,

Finish my iniquity, finish my vanity,

That is how those wounds would heal,

This is how you will destroy my heart's sin chamber,

Let me always praise you like I did today,

Wake me up if my soul falls into slumber"

Amen!

Prayer 36: Prayer for respect

"My God, show me and teach me how to model respect for my children, open my eyes to the areas in my life where I can be more respectful. May my children show proper respect to everyone as your word commands as I seek You in this area of my life."

Amen!

Prayer 37: Prayer for patience

"Lord, I am seeking your peace and your patience. I want to learn to wait patiently for you to bring your answers to my prayers. I want to cooperate with your plans for me. Thank you for assuring me that your plans for me are good."

Amen!

Prayer 38: Prayer for understanding

"Please fill my heart with understanding
May I always seek to contemplate
What somebody may be suffering
Before I jump to any conclusions
Because I know that you never cease
To pardon me"

Amen!

Prayer 39: Prayer for piety

"O my Lord, teach me piety. May my prayers levitate to Heaven In the form of melodies and rainbows; bless me with a life of contemplation that will enrich my soul eternally. You are my Paragon of pious devotion!"

Prayer 40: Prayer for Honesty

"Oh God, shine on me,

the holy light of honesty,

so that my soul is no more rusty,

bless me with the virtue of loyalty,

of compassion, affection and nobility,

let your sunlight of truthfulness shine on me,

let me be a moon for world's eternal harmony."

Amen!

Prayer 41: Prayer – asking for God's Favor in Moses' way

"Now therefore, if I have found favor in your sight, please show me now your ways, that I may know you in order to find favor in your sight."

Amen!

Prayer 42: Prayer for Chastity

"Help us all to keep the commitments that we have made to You. Help us to stay pure for that one special person that will one day be our husband or wife. Give us the strength to remain pure and let us always remember that the reward for purity will be well worth it."

Amen!

Prayer 43: Prayer for Love

"O my God, I love you above all things with my whole heart and soul, because you are all good and worthy of all my love. I love my neighbor as myself for the love of you. I forgive all who have injured me and I ask pardon of those whom I have injured."
Amen!

Prayer 44: Prayer for guarding me through Guardian Angel

"O My God, O My Lord!
Let your Angel, my guardian dear,
to whom Your love entrusts me here.
Ever this day be at my side to light,
to guard to rule and guide."
Amen!

Prayer 45: Prayer for justice

"O Lord we pray,

We pray for justice to prevail,

Vindicate those who are suffering injustice,

Show the unjust people right path,

The path of balance and the path of Jesus,

The path that you want us to follow,

in each and every dealing of our life.

We pray for mercy to all those who are victims

To injustice that is happening anywhere in your kingdom

We pray for peace to prevail,

Let every heart be your home,

And every house be your place of worship."

Amen!

Part 2

Prayers for Family and Similar Kinds of Relationships

Prayer 46: Prayer for the family

"Lord, behold our family here assembled.
We thank you for this place in which we dwell,
for the love that unites us,
for the peace accorded to us this day,
for the hope with which we expect the morrow;
for the health, the work, the food and the bright
skies
that make our lives delightful;
for our friends in all parts of the earth."

Amen!

Prayer 47: Prayer for the unborn child

"Our Lord, our creator,

You are the sustainer of all life

We pray to you to be a protector,

Of this unborn child which will come to life

Only as per your will and as per your order,

A seed grows into a tree and a bird has its voice."

Amen!

Prayer 48: Children's prayer for their parents

"Beloved Lord!

Thank you for bestowing us with a loving mother,

Thank you for bestowing us with a caring father,

Bless our parents with your holy grace,

Enrich their hearts with thy pure love,

Grant then what they cherish for,

Guard them with your holy angels as they do for us,

Forgive their tiniest sins and smallest mistakes,

Fill their lives with eternal joy,

May they never leave the path of Jesus Christ,

Bless them with health in body and mind even when they are old,

Bless us with the opportunity to serve them when they are old,

Just like they cared for us when we were helpless babies"

Amen!

Prayer 49: Parents prayer to their children

"My dear God, you are the one who bestowed me these children

You have been my savior, be their savior too

You have been my guide, guide them to the light

Supply in me whatever is lacking, to take their responsibility and foster them with love

Strengthen my kids to face the world with determination

Build their skills so that they make their own way and follow their passion

Make them mentally strong and physically powerful

Protect them from the bad eyes of the enemy

Let them be an epitome of love

Let them live their life like the Jesus guided us

Fill in their hearts the love of you and Jesus,

Help them grow in knowledge every single day,

Protect them, guide them and never let them go astray"

Amen!

Prayer 50: Parents prayer to their children (2)

"Loving God,

Thank you for the gift of our children.

Help us to set boundaries for them,
and yet encourage them to explore.
Give us the strength and courage to treat
each day as a fresh start.

May our children come to know you, the one true
God,
and Jesus Christ, whom you have sent.

May your nourishing power help them to grow
in faith, hope, and love,
so they may know peace, truth, and goodness."

Amen!

Prayer 51: Parents prayer to their children (3)

"My God, the creator of mankind,

You have bestowed me with these children,

And given me their responsibility and an opportunity of parenthood,

Which some people cherish their whole life to have,

I thank you for this charge, thank you for this blessing.

Help me with your grace and power,

So that I may be able to happily fulfill this stewardship and sacred duty

Teach me ways to make these children obedient unto thee

Hold my hand whenever I am helpless to show them the right path or guide them to light

Make me gentle unto them and make them sincere and obedient,

Help me prepare myself as well as these flowers prepare for that eternal life,

The life that you have promised,

So that I might live forever with them,

in the company of holy saints and angles in your heaven."

Amen!

Prayer 52: Parents prayer to their teenage daughter

"Oh my Lord,

You have blessed me with a beautiful daughter,

I can't ever stop to thank you for that,

My Lord, it just seems like yesterday when she was a child,

Now she is a teenager and growing into a young woman,

Thank you for the happiness and joy

that she has brought us through all these years,

Oh Lord, give me wisdom to deal patiently with her irritations and needs,

her frustrations and her dreams.

I pray to you my Lord,

That with every passing year,

She and I grow closer to each other,

And we both grow closer to you.

I wish she becomes the person she wants to be,

the person who is close to you through her work, deeds and actions.

I pray to you to bless her with true friends, friends she can trust,

Friends I can trust for her to be with,

Friends who would make her grow spiritually, mentally and make her progress

Oh God, guard her and help her in all the decisions she takes, in all the choices she makes,

Help her prosper and be a good person,

And let her face all the phases of her life boldly as she grows into adulthood."

Amen!

Prayer 53: Parents prayer to their teenage son

"Oh my Lord,

You have blessed me with a handsome son,

I can't ever stop to thank you for that,

My Lord, it just seems like yesterday when he was a child,

Now he is a teenager and growing into a young man,

Thank you for the happiness and joy

that he has brought us through all these years,

Oh Lord, give me wisdom to deal patiently with his irritations and needs,

his aggression and his dreams.

I pray to you my Lord,

That with every passing year,

He and I grow closer to each other,

And we both grow closer to you.

I wish he becomes the person he wants to be,

the person who is close to you through his work, deeds and actions.

I pray to you to bless him with true friends, friends he can trust,

Friends I can trust for him to be with,

Friends who would make him grow spiritually, mentally and make her progress

Oh God, guard him and help him in all the decisions he takes, in all the choices he makes,

Help him prosper and be a good person,

And let him face all the phases of her life boldly as he grows into adulthood."

Amen!

Prayer 54: Prayer for sisters

"I thank you God, for blessing me with such a darling sister,

And thank you for all those wonderful times we have spend together,

Thank you for all the encouragement she gave me in times of distress and hardships,

I pray that she remains away from all kinds of hardships,

I pray that she is never in distress,

I pray that her every wish is fulfilled, that she always remains happy, that she is in the best of her health always and may your hand of protection be always on her head."

Amen!

Day 55: Prayer for brothers

"I thank you God, for blessing me with such a wonderful brother,

And thank you for all those wonderful times we have spend together,

Thank you for all the help he provided me in hard times,

I pray that he remains away from all kinds of hardships,

I pray that he is never in distress,

I pray that his every dream comes true, that he always remains happy, that he is in the best of his health always and may your hand of protection be always on his head."

Amen!

Prayer 56: Wedding prayers

"My dear Lord,

We thank you so much for this day,

The day of our union,

The day of our marriage,

This is indeed the most beautiful day,

As you have cherished our desires,

To be together forever,

You have united two souls,

To be glued to each other through the gum of love,

Of compassion and affection,

We pray that your blessings will always find their way to our home,

The peace will prevail in our home,

There will be joy and happiness in our life,

We will always live together in unity, no matter what,

We will be woven with the stitches of understanding, love and care,

May your presence be always felt by both of us,

As we are feeling it right here, right now!"

Amen!

Prayer 57: Parents prayer to their baby

"Dear Lord

Thank you for delivering this child of ours safely into this world,

We ask you to shower your best blessings on this little life,

Protect this little one, guard this little one,

Bless this little flower with the knowledge of Jesus Christ

as he/she grows through various phases of life,"

Amen!

Prayer 58: Prayer for fathers

"Dear beloved God!

I feel very blessed to have a father like him,

I thank you for placing me in this loving family,

Thank you for all the joy and fun we have shared through all these years,

Thank you for the things I have learnt from my father,

I pray to you Oh my Lord,

That my father remains in best of his health always,

That he is blessed with everything he wants.

That you make me and my obedience towards him, one of the reasons of his happiness,

Thank you God, for bestowing me this father who,

Made me strong in our times of difficulty,

Gave me wisdom in the troublesome times,

Showed me how to be truthful when I used to make a mistake,

I pray to you to grant him peace of mind and physical strength,"

Amen!

Prayer 59: Prayer for mothers

"Dear beloved God!

I feel very blessed to have a mother like her,

I thank you for placing me in this loving family,

Thank you for all the joy and fun we have shared through all these years,

Thank you for the love and care I received from my mother,

I pray to you Oh my Lord,

That my mother remains in best of her health always,

That she is blessed with everything she wants.

That you make me and my affection towards her, one of the reasons of her happiness,

Thank you God, for bestowing me this mother who,

Carried me in her womb for nine long months,

Cared for me when I was a little child,

Protected me from every bad thing in the world,

I pray to you to grant her peace of mind and physical strength,"

Amen!

Prayer 60: Prayers for Marriage

"Beloved Lord,

Thank you for all the blessings that we received from everyone,

Thank you for uniting two families together,

Thank you for bestowing me this gracious soul-mate,

who is truly a wonderful gift from you

Dear Lord,

I pray to you that we as a couple remain united forever,

That our souls get closer and closer day by day,

That we develop a sense of great understanding between us,

that we face each phase of our life boldly together,

that we enjoy each other's company."

Amen!

Prayer 61: Prayer for spouse

"My Loving God,

Thank you so much for the spouse,

That you have blessed me with,

And I pray that with each and every passing day,

We continue to grow together, hand in hand,

Grow in love and compassion,

I pray that our union may be filled with love, filled with trust,

and you, Oh my Lord, kindly supply our lives with a continuous supply of your grace,

fill our hearts with peace,

Oh Lord, make our hearts cheerful,

Make us forgive each other's mistakes,

Make us each other's strength,

Bless us with a natural compassion for each other."

Amen!

Prayer 62: Prayer for a Friend

"Dear God,

I thank you so much for filling my life with a wonderful friend,

Thank you so much for this friendship bond between us,

Lord, I pray this blessing of friendship flourish like that of David and Jonathan,

Like that of Naomi with Ruth,

Lord, I pray that my friend's life is filled with your grace, your love, your protection,

and your choicest blessings.

I pray that my friend grows in knowledge of our beloved Jesus,

Knowledge of the hereafter,

and knowledge of you.

Strengthen and keep us united always, and let us be increasingly rooted to Your glory,"

Amen!

Prayer 63: Prayer for love

"Dear Loving Lord,
Fill my life with truth and love,
Help me recognize the helpless and needy,
Encourage me to help and love them,
Make me just to your people,
Make me love people for your sake,
Let me receive love from your people too,
Let me receive love from you!"
Amen!

Part 3

Prayers for Different Activities and Events

Prayer 64: Travel prayer

"Oh creator,
Be our protector,
be our guide,
for this journey,
Keep us away from accidents,
Keep us away from untoward events,
Keep our health safe and sound,
Keep our minds alert,
Make us enjoy this wonderful journey,
Help us in times of difficulty,
Keep us mindful of your love and presence,"
Amen!

Prayer 65: Prayers before study time

"O powerful God,

I pray to you that your light of knowledge enters into my heart and mind,

Bless me with the grace to use this knowledge wisely,

Let me excel in all my endeavors.

Bless me with fortitude and perseverance.

Braoden my heart, so that it accumulates all the knowledge that I gather,

Help my memory, so that I remember the things I learn,

Make me recall perfectly what I learn and memorize,

Guide me while I am reading; guide me while I am writing,

Guide me when I am listening to my teacher,

Guide me while I am appearing in the test,

Guide me during an interview,

Fill my mind with correct concepts and make those consolidated right in there."

Amen!

Prayer 66: Prayers before study time (2)

"O Lord,

help me in settling back to my daily routine of school,

give me a heart that has a burning desire to learn,

a brain that has a wonderful power of retention and understanding,

the skills that I easily apply what I learn to my life and to the problems,

O God,

Hold my hand and never let me go astray,

Keep me on the track and increase me in knowledge day by day,

Let me make my parents proud,

Let me achieve the highest ranks,

in the eyes of people and in your eyes too."

Amen!

Prayer 67: Prayers before any Game/Sport

"O heavenly God,
You have created me in the best body,

I thank you for all the strength that you bestowed me,

Let me pursue excellence during this game,

And enjoy every moment of it,

Protect me from all harm and injury,

Fill my heart with true spirit of sportsmanship,

And provide me
with the endurance and stamina that is required to excel."

Amen!

Part 4

Prayers for Important Moments in Time

Prayer 68: Morning Offering

"O my Lord,

Thank you for this new day of my life,

I am offering you my prayers,
from the core of my heart,

From the depth of my soul,

I offer you my joys, my sufferings and my works,

of this new day,

I am offering them for the reparation of my sins and
for the salvation of my soul"

Amen!

Prayer 69: Morning Prayer

"O my dear God,

O my Loving Lord,

I am offering you on this day,

All that I do and all that I say,
I am offering it with all that was done
by Jesus on this earth

Protect me and guide me,

throughout the day."
Amen.

Prayer 70: Evening Prayer

"O my God,

O my Loving Lord,

Thank you for this day,

as this day is done.
I pray to you to send your angels,

To guard our night,

So that we sleep and they bless our rest."

Amen!

Prayer 71: Prayer before Meals

"O creator,

O sustainer,

O provider of everything,

Bless us and the food we are about to receive,

From your immense bounty,

In your name we begin"

Amen!

Prayer 72: Prayer after Meals

"O sustainer of all creatures,
We thank you for all that you provided us,
Keep providing us always from your treasures,
We are always be grateful to you,
Without your help nothing is possible."
Amen!

Prayer 73: Bed-time prayers

"I am thanking you with the feelings of satisfaction,
With your grace we are born,
and with your grace we die and reach our eternal
destination
I lay myself down with your name;
and I rise with Your Name,
And if you take away my you,
I pray that you have your mercy on it ,
If You send it back then I pray for your protection,
in the same way that you protect your righteous
men and women!"
Amen!

Prayer 74: Prayer at times when you need real strength - Samson's Prayer

"O my all powerful Lord,
O Almighty God,
I pray to you to remember me
and I pray that you strengthen me"
Amen!

Prayer 75: Prayer during difficult times

"O God,
My heart rejoices in you
my horn is exalted in you
there is no savior beside you
there is no one as strong as you
there is no Rock like you my God
there is no one as mighty as you,
bless me with strength and might"
Amen!

Prayer 76: Harvest-time prayers

"Dear God,

We thank you for all the nice things you provide us every day,

We thank you for the food you gave us every day,

We remember those who don't have even enough to fill their belly with one meal,

who suffer due to the greed of others,

We ask you to bless them,

Help us share our harvest with the world in a fair manner

so that there is no more hunger left in the world,

there is no more starvation in the world,

and our brothers and sisters of the world feed themselves

like we do by your grace."

Amen!

Prayer 77: Prayer when you are afflicted with an infectious disease- The Leper's Prayer

"Lord, you are clean,
You love cleanliness
You are the healer
You send Jesus to us who was the healer
Heal me O my Lord and make me clean."
Amen!

Prayer 78: Prayer when you have to take a life-changing decision

"O my Lord, I beseech you for I am in a dilemma,

I tried a lot using the conscious mind you gave me to make this decision,

Yet I failed, so I am turning to you, and asking your favour,

to let Your holy ear be attentive for me

and Your holy eyes open to hear,

my prayer and help me out in taking the right decision at this moment"

Amen!

Prayer 79: Holiday prayer

"O my dear Lord,

We thank You for these holiday times

We thank you for all the excitement and wonder that these times engender in us

We thank you for all the grace and goodness that you pour in our lives

We are remembering you in these good times, and O our God, we want your presence in our lives in all times, good or bad, because you are the one who loves us multiple times than our mother, you created us and you are our sustainer.

Thank you for everything our Lord

May we always keep praising your glory"

Amen!

Prayer 80: Birthday prayer

"O Loving God,

thank you for this day of my life

thank you for all the gifts and cards,

Thank you for all the love tokens I am receiving,

*This reminds me of how much I am being loved,
how important is my existence,*

the existence that you brought to life.

Let me vanish all my vanity and iniquity today,

Let me be humble with each passing year

*I thank you for all the care you took of me through
all these years through various sources,*

*I commit this birthday, O my Lord, to you and only
you!*

I want more of your love

I want more of your guidance"

Amen!

Prayer 81: Prayer when you feel helpless

"My Lord,

No one is besides You who can help me,

No one is besides you who can harm me,

Help me O my sustainer!

For I am feeling helpless now,

help me in this battle between those who have no strength,

and those who are powerful,

yet not powerful than you.

Your strength is greater than everything else in the universe

In you I put my trust,

Help me my Lord, you are definitely the best"

Amen!

Prayer 82: Prayer for invocation of the dead and on All Souls day

"We pray to thee our Lord,
Grant an eternal rest unto them,
O Lord,
Let your everlasting light of mercy shine upon them,
May they rest in peace"
Amen!

Prayer 83: Praying when your heart feels sinful but you need God's help

"My iniquities testifying against me
But O my merciful Lord
Act for Thy name's sake
And help your servant!"
Amen!

Part 5

Prayers against Various Forms of Sin

Prayer 84: Act of Contrition

"O My Merciful Lord,
I am ashamed before you,

with all my heart,

for all my sins,

I have sinned and I admit it,

Sinned against you,

Sinned in choosing to do wrong,

Sinned in failing to do good,

I have failed in following your path of love,

I have sinned in going against you,

whom I should love above everything else
But now I intend firmly,

and make a commitment,

that with your help,
I will do penance,
I won't do any sin any more,
I would avoid whatever it is that leads me to sin.
O God of Jesus, O God of Mary,

have mercy on me , have mercy on me."

Amen!

Prayer 85: Prayer to turn away from sin

"O dear God,

I have been a sinner by breaking your laws,

I have allowed these sins to separate me from you,

Now I want to abandon these sins,

I want to say sorry for all bad that I have done,

I want to turn my back to this sinful life that I have lived,

Forgive me and help me in turning away from each and everything associated with my sins,

For the rest of my life, I will always obey you,

Please God, mend my mettle"

Amen!

Prayer 86: Supplication prayer

O Lord,

I am crying unto Thee,

Hear my voice and my plea

Let thine ears listen to my supplication attentively,

With you is plentiful redemption, with you there is mercy

Forgive me O Lord, Forgive me

Amen!

Prayer 87: Supplication – a cry of sinner

"Be merciful to me, I am a sinner

Take me out of sins, I am a sinner

You are the forgiver and I am a sinner

Make me pure again, I am a sinner

I will cry, I will continue to weep,

For achieving your forgiveness, I will continue to plead,

I will continue to supplicate, until I get your answer,

that O my servant, O my lover,

I have forgiven you; you are no longer a sinner!"

Amen!

Prayer 88: Prayer against drug addiction, drunkenness and alcoholism

"We pray for all those, O our Lord,

who are suffering in any way, due to alcoholic addiction or abuse,

especially the ones who we know personally.

We pray that in Your mercy and grace,

You would do a lot to improve their habits and lives,

And enable them to break free of their devastating addiction,

And free their minds from all sort of evil stress,

that might have led them to resort to addiction,

and we pray that may all of them restore their faith in you and Jesus,

and follow his path on earth"

Amen!

Prayer 89: Prayer against adultery

"O my dear God,

I pray for my spouse,

That may the evil spirit of adultery leave him/her,

That may he/she lead from now onwards a pure and spiritual life,

The life that you would be pleased with,

The life that brings life to our relationship again as it used to have before"

Amen!

Prayer 90: Prayer against gluttony

"O Lord the forgiver,

I ask for your forgiveness,

For my drunkenness,

for my gluttony,

for my all sorts of addictions.

Help me through thy grace,

To shun all these sinful acts,

And come back to your path of peace and harmony.

Amen!

Prayer 91: Prayer against temptations

"O my Lord,

You are most merciful,

Free my heart from the irresistible temptations of the world,

The temptations that take this servant of yours miles away from your love,

Make me a worthy person for your love and for your heaven to dwell forever."

Amen!

Part 6

Prayers for Righteousness and Salvation

Prayer 92: Prayer for salvation

"I thank You my Lord,

For you opened my internal eyes,

To envision your purpose of creating me,

And getting to know the importance of focusing more on eternity and hereafter,

Make me faithful to share this message of holy salvation with others,

who have curtain before their eyes"

Amen!

Prayer 93: Prayer for salvation (2)

"My God, my creator, my sustainer,

I repent of all that I have done wrong in your eyes,

As you the knower of secrets in the heart,

You are the knower of intention behind actions,

I repent for everything done wrong,

Knowingly or unknowingly,

I pray to you to make me holy,

And set me apart for you.

I seek to life this life that you have given me, only and only for you"

Amen!

Prayer 94: Prayer for reconciliation

"O Lord,

Bless us with a peaceful spirit,

Bless us with a desire to be reconciled with each other."

Amen!

Prayer 95: Prayer for reconciliation (2)

"My Loving Lord,

Make us your ambassadors of reconciliation,

Reconcile me to my loved ones,

Make us humble so that we don't be egoistic in relationships,

Make us gentle so that we don't become fierce at each other's mistakes,

Warm our hearts so that we become embodiment of love on this earth"

Amen!

Part 7

Prayers for Others in Difficult Situations

Prayer 96: Prayers for the poor and needy

"O Lord,

Help our ears to listen to the cries of the needy,

Encourage us to help them from the bounties you have bestowed us with,
Help us raise voice against the injustice happening anywhere in your kingdom,

Help us speak out the words of love and acceptance to them,

Make us your feet to walk beside those who are in need,

Make us your hands to feed, shelter and clothe them,

Hear our prayer so that there is no one hungry in this world,

Hear our prayer so that we establish harmony in the world!"

Amen!

Prayer 97: Prayer for the sick

"Oh Lord,

You are merciful,

You are healer,

You are the one, who bestows good health,

You are the everlasting hope of those who have faith in you,

Restore the health of this sick servant of yours,

Clear away all the illness,

Heal away all the pain,

So that he/she might rise again and express his/her heart filled gratitude,

Because you are the one who deserves our thanks,

You are the one to whom we pray,

You gave Jesus the powers to raise dead and dying,

You make this sick servant rise again"

Amen!

Prayer 98: Prayers for those in last agony

"O kind Lord,
you are compassionate towards the souls,
I pray to you to wash away all the sins,

Heal all this pain,

Of those in agony,

And who are going to die this day."

Amen!

Prayer 99: Prayers for the bereaved

"O Creator,
You are the God of consolation,
in your mercy for us,

and in your limitless love for us,

turn this dark shadow of of death
into a bright sunlight of new life.

Show your love to your servants,

in their sorrow.

O Lord,

Be our strength and be our refuge,

Lift us from the trench of this miserable grief
to the light and peace of your holy presence.

Bless the departed soul with your mercy"

Amen!

Prayer 100: Prayers for the Distraught and Anguished

O Lord,

We are calling upon You

In these bad times of sorrow,

That to bear these heavy burdens on our shoulders,

You bestow us with strength,

And make us feel the warmth of your love and affection

O lord, let us face these hardships easily and with a smile,

As it shows how much faith we have in you,

For after every hardship, you have created ease,

We trust in you,

We have faith in you,

Amen!

Conclusion

Prayers are important in our daily lives. There are millions of Christians out there who struggle on daily basis not knowing how to pray. Thus, having this book which provides great powerful prayers helps Christians to strengthen their faith through effective prayers. You too can benefit from this. I hope you have benefited. Share it with others in these prayers so that many can be able to effectively communicate with the Lord through prayers.

Finally, if you enjoyed this book, then I'd like to ask you for a favor, would you be kind enough to leave a review for this book on Amazon? It'd be greatly appreciated!

http://www.amazon.com/dp/B017MW4IBA/

Thank you for downloading and reading this book.

Made in the USA
Monee, IL
12 May 2022

96265618R00059